INDUSTRIAL ROTHERHAM
IN PICTURES

Industrial Rotherham

IN PICTURES

PAUL WALTERS & GILES BREARLEY

WHARNCLIFFE PUBLISHING

First Published in 1998 by
Wharncliffe Publishing
an imprint of
Pen and Sword Books Limited,
47 Church Street, Barnsley,
South Yorkshire. S70 2AS

Copyright © Wharncliffe Publishing 1998

For up-to-date information on other titles produced under the
Wharncliffe imprint, please telephone or write to:

    Wharncliffe Publishing
    FREEPOST
    47 Church Street
    Barnsley
    South Yorkshire S70 2BR
    Telephone (24 hours): 01226 - 734555

ISBN: 1-871647-51-7

A CIP catalogue record of this book is available from the
British Library

Front cover: Molten iron being poured into a Kaldo unit at Parkgate. 1964
Back cover: British Oxygen distribution centre at Aldwarke. 1964

Printed in Great Britain by
St. Edmundsbury Press, Bury St. Edmunds, Suffolk.

Cover Design by Carly Spark

INTRODUCTION

Michael Walters 1933 to 1994.

Michael Walters was born in January 1933 and raised at his parents home in Mexborough in the industrial heartland of South Yorkshire.

The son of a commercial photographer who worked for the Daily Mirror during World War 2, Michael developed an interest in photography at an early age.

Educated at Mexborough Grammar school and Worksop college, Michael joined the Army where he rose to the rank of Captain in the Royal Army Ordnance Corp. After leaving the army in 1955, he set up his own photographic company, working on a great many of the industrial projects that shaped the area and it's people. His reputation grew and M.T. Walters and Associates was to develop into one of Europe's most prestigious photographic companies, with assignments in such places as Malawi, Trinidad & Tobago, Jamaica, Canada and the United States in addition to numerous European countries.

He developed his own special lighting techniques which were particularly sucessful in capturing the inherent drama of steel making. As a result of this, his reputation grew and he worked intensively in the steel yards and mills of Sheffield and Rotherham to produce what is believed to be the most comprehensive photographic record available of life in the area's steel works. A small selection of these can be seen in the Parkgate section of this

book and these give an insight into a once great industry and the people who worked in it.

Of course Michael did not confine his work to steel making, with clients as diverse as Danish Bacon, and the National Coal Board, his work covered a wide spectrum and in 1986 he was awarded the National Architectura Award by the British Institute of Professional Photographers for his shot of the Reform Club in London's Pall Mall.

During his career, Michael amassed a collection of some 240,000 negatives, this collection is now the Michael Walters Industrial Archive.

His own interests were centred around the Industrial Revolution and ecclesiastical architecture which he recorded on his travels and planned to make into a book when he retired from professional life. Unfortunately he was never able to achieve this as his health deteriorated and sadly, he died in October 1994 at the age of 61.

Paul Walters.

THE MICHAEL WALTERS INDUSTRIAL ARCHIVE

The photographs featured in this book are available as 10″x 8″ prints mounted in a high quality frame, at a cost of £18.00 each including postage and packaging. To place your order, please write with cheque payable to:

Worldwide Photography Ltd.

at: The Studios, Dolcliffe Road, Mexborough. South Yorkshire S64 9AZ
Telephone: (01709) 582474

One of the many footbridges erected over the M1, this bridge crosses the motorway on the stretch between Rotherham and Barnsley. As can be seen, there was still much work to be done before the motorway was ready for opening. *13356 / 13358. 3/8/67.*

Commissioned by Rank Xerox, this photograph shows British Steel staff using the latest in copying machines. 6387. 3/8/62.

All Saints Parish Church undergoing renovation. The scaffolders skills can be seen developed to a fine art in this photograph.
The church dates back to the 12th Century. The current building was constructed on the same site as an earlier Norman church. A visit to the inside of the church is highly recommended as it incorporates fine stonework and many splendid memorials.
33406. 23/3/73.

Mr and Mrs Claxton about to cross the threshold of the brand new Sprite caravan, which they won in the Brooke Bond Tea promotion sponsored by ASDA supermarkets. *32485. 1/9/72.*

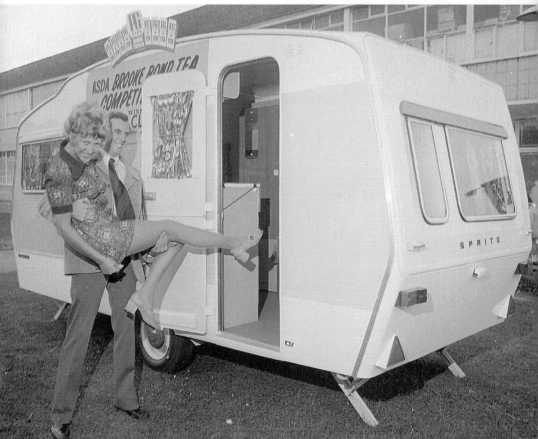

The car park at th new ASDA store i Rotherham. Many of the vehicles in the car park are now collectors items. One wonders about th motor scooter wit the Mateus Rose crate on the carrier! *20836. 27/3/69.*

The ASDA supermarket, originally situated on Eastwood Trading Estate, with shoppers waiting to make their purchases. As can be seen, the store is decked out with baloons and bunting, despite the photograph being taken in late March. Could this be an early 'event' to draw still more customers into the store? 20848. 27/3/69.

SUGG Sports on Wellgate. One of the few shops still trading from the same premises, though the range of goods has altered from general leisure goods such as chess boards and television sets in this photograph, to now being totally sports orientated. Note the exotic antenna on the roof.
4570. November 1960.

Construction work in progress at Wade Court, Ship Hill, by Wades builders. Merryweather and Corbett, now Merryweather Auctioneers, still trade from these premises.
The Rover car in front of the building under construction, would definitely be a classic today.
The square where this property stands has recently undergone extensive renovations and is now one of the more attractive areas of the town. Wades traded until the early 1990's.
5690. 27/3/62.

Photograph comissioned by T.C. Harrison, local agent for Ford trucks. This was the latest truck purchased by Mason Brothers, Hauliers, of Rotherham. *15247. 28/12/67.*

A variation on the old book title, 'Three Men in a Bath' on this occasion, Stan Laurel, portrayed by Ted Smith, seems to have wandered out of the Hollywood studio and into Mike Walters'.
This was a promotional studio set and the photograph was used in a Heatons Baths advertising campaign. Heatons manufactured baths in Rotherham for many years. The buildings they once occupied now have a number of uses, including housing a night club. *10756. 18/11/66.*

Another advertising photograph for Heatons. On this occasion featuring the Imperial combined bath and shower unit. The model so demurely wrapped in the bath towel was a local girl. *10629. 21/10/66.*

The British Oxygen Company was established in 1886. The large and constant demand for oxygen by the iron and steel industries made the Rotherham plant a thriving concern. This photograph portrays technicians using vibration sensing equipment inside the plant. Vibration is an integral part of the production process, but it can cause dangerous fractures in pipelines and vessels. Regular testing is an essential safety precaution. *11166. 20/1/66.*

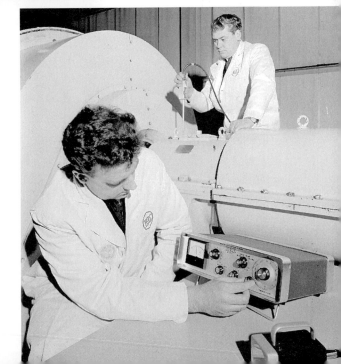

Scrap metal being categorised and baled at the Edgar Allen scrap plant. The company was founded in 1868 as manufacturers of special steels for use in the manufacture of tramway points, crossings, files, saws and fine bladed tools. The headquarters of the company were at the Imperial Steelworks in Sheffield, which covered an area of 35 acres. The Rotherham plant acted as a recycling centre for the company.
9158. 11/5/65.

Burghwallis House once a splendid private residence, is situated below the hospital on Doncaster Road and has for many years provided prestigious offices for various companies. It is currently occupied by the firms 'Health Care' and accountancy firm of 'Rooke & Co.'
6132. 24/5/62.

These photographs, taken for Woodall Duckham Construction Co Ltd, show Carr House gas works in Rotherham during the later stages of construction. This plant is situated off Ginhouse Lane, near the Barbot Hall Industrial Estate. The plant is today operated by Laporte Industries. *2154 & 2155. 12/9/61.*

The window of the Rotherham East Midlands Gas Board shop during one of the many promotions during the early 1960's aimed at coaxing householders to switch from coal to gas. In this case, featuring the Ascot water heater, many of which are still in use today. Technically these water heaters were the forerunners of the modern combi boiler. 5095. 29/6/61.

The aftermath of the collapse of a Lima type crane on the S.P.E.A.R. construction site in Templeborough. The collapse was the result of the crane attempting to lift an excessively heavy weight. It is not known if there were any injuries as a result of the accident. *5334. 12/9/61.*

These four photographs show the construction of the Walls Ice Cream Companys' new distribution depot under construction. Comissioned by Norwest Construction, the shot below right shows how close to local residential areas the plant was. *2248, 2278 & 2293. 24/5/57.*

These photographs show the new grain silo under construction at the mills of Joseph Rank ltd. The daytime shot was taken from atop the old grain silo prior to demolition, while the nighttime shot serves to illustrate how serious were the penalty clauses on the builders for late completion.
18035 & 18036. 4/7/68.

The Joseph Rank company started life in London in 1875 and by 1932, had four mills in London and others in Hull, Barry in South Wales and Birkenhead. The Hovis company also began in London and steadily expanded northwards. During the 1970's the two companies merged to become Rank Hovis McDougall. This mill has been further extended since the merger and is now known as Town Mills.

ASDA shoppers doing the rounds just before decimalisation. The stores had a much more utilitarian look in those days, but just look at those prices.
1/- equals 5p today !
20840, 20844 & 20845.
27/3/69.

Three new additions to the transport fleet of Bryan Thorpe Haulage.
This company went into liquidation some years ago, but the family tradition is carried on
by Mr Martin Thorpe who operates from Mexborough under the name of
K.T.S. (Rotherham) Ltd. *32534. 1/9/72.*

One of the more diminutive members of the Thorpe Transport fleet. Bryan Thorpe raced
this stock car at local events in the early 70's. His sucess rate is not recorded !
C32536. 14/9/72.

Repair and modernisation work being carried out at Silverwood colliery by Norwest Construction Ltd. The massive chimney base of the steam winding mechanism can be clearly seen. *995. 1/12/55.*

In the spring of 1955, the surface facilities were further enhanced by extensions to a number of buildings. This was necessary to cope with the demands of steadily increasing output from the pit. *2455. 3/5/55.*

The upgrading of the winding house is almost complete at Silverwood colliery. The company involved in this project was Harbour and General Works Ltd.
During the early 1960's, many of the South Yorkshire collieries were improved. Their coal preparation plants in particular were the subject of considerable investment by the National Coal Board. *4062. 4/3/60.*

An aerial photograph of improvement work in progress at Silverwood colliery.
As can be clearly seen, work is still in progress. *4063. 4/3/60.*

Workers brave the cold to carry out emergency reconstruction work at Silverwood colliery. We assume the railway track was not used while this work was going on. Note the absence of silencers on the pneumatic drills and a seemingly glorious disregard for workers safety during these operations. No doubt some of these younger civil engineers will be filing claims for 'vibration white finger' *994. 15/12/54.*

These photographs form part of a series of twenty taken for the National Coal Board. They show the site of a fatal accident at Silverwood colliery. The victim is portrayed by a volunteer. In the accident, a surface worker was found dead at the side of the track, having been hit by a train. The full series of photographs was used at the subsequent inquest.

1660 & 1662. 2/7/56.

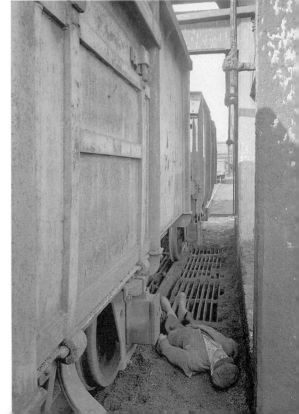

Les Saunders, as usual in good spirits, selling copies of the industry magazine Coal, to NUM and NACOD's members on their way to and from Thurcroft colliery.`
3890. 6/11/59.

Work in progress on the Coal Preparation Plant at Maltby colliery. The contractors, J.L. Kier & Co Ltd, completed the project to improve the plant in 1961. *4036. 23/2/60.*

This overhead photograph of the coal feed hopper under construction. The shot shows the massive steel reinforcement necessary in the structure. *4037. 23/2/60.*

This intriguing photograph was taken in the loft of the Wickersley home of Mr T.H. Watford. Clearly Mr Watford was a keen and competent railway modeller. We understand that the entire layout including all the buildings and scenery where of his own construction. Though this is the type of model railway layout that young boys dream of, it only goes to prove that railway modelling is not for kids! *Unnumbered photograph. 8/9/60.*

In this photograph can be seen Mr George Schonut, great grandson of the original Schonut who originated in the German city of Obenhof. The family settled in Mexborough at some time before World War 1. Despite a certain amount of persecution stemming from their German name and origins, George's father refused to anglicise the family name. The butchery business started by his grandfather flourished through three generations and traded both as retailers and wholesale suppliers to other butchers in the area. *1955. (From boxed set).*

One of the first events held at the newly constructed Leisure Centre was the Rawmarsh Trades Fair. Local Trades Fairs were seen as essential for the promotion of local manufactures in the 1960's and most industrial towns put them on. In this photograph we see part of the solid fuel fight back against the energetic promotion of gas as an economical and clean fuel. *14601. 9/11/67.*

The Woolworths premises in Parkgate. The presence of a 'Woolies' was often seen as a sign that a town had 'made it', during the years following World War 2. The premises have since been vacated by Woolworths and a number of tenant organisations, including the Yorkshire Bank, have come and gone. The Midland Bank premises to the right are currently empty but otherwise little has changed. The cables for the 'Trackless' busses can be seen over the road way. These resembled a normal bus apart from the contact arms on the roof which contacted with the power cables. The Trackless' finished service 27th March, 1961, with some being sold on for service in San Francisco. *2273. 23/6/57.*

An advertising photograph taken for the Brooks Damp Proof Course Machine Company. The property being treated is on Furlong Road.

Brooks were in at the beginning of the boom in injection damp proofing, which introduced a damp proof course to properties which were built without this essential protection against rising damp. *2381. 8/10/57.*

As a promotion, the Don and Dearne Television Company decided to mount a 'Bride of the Year' competition and bring a nationally known star to Goldthorpe. The T.V. and recording star Wee Willie Harris was the star chosen to present the prize to the winning bride.

Wee Willie Harris was one of the crop of early 50's rock & roll stars to be discovered while performing at the then famous 2 I's Club in London. Wee Willie started his rock & roll career as Wee Jock Harris, but Wee Willie was seen as a more saleable name. He is five feet tall and in his younger days had a shock of red hair, which he frequently dyed bright pink. Both on and off stage he wore well cut but extremely colourful clothes, favouring pink, green and blue. His socks also became a fashion statement with multi coloured rings round them and different colours on each foot !

His first hit record was Two by One, but following appearances on the television show Six Five Special, he shot to fame with his rendition of 'Wild One'. He was often billed as the British Jerry Lee Lewis. Wee Willie has retired from the entertainment world but is still the ebullient character he always was. *2584. 14/3/58.*

This photograph taken by Mike, shows the winning couple leaving the Methodist Church on Doncaster Road. *2584. 14/3/58.*

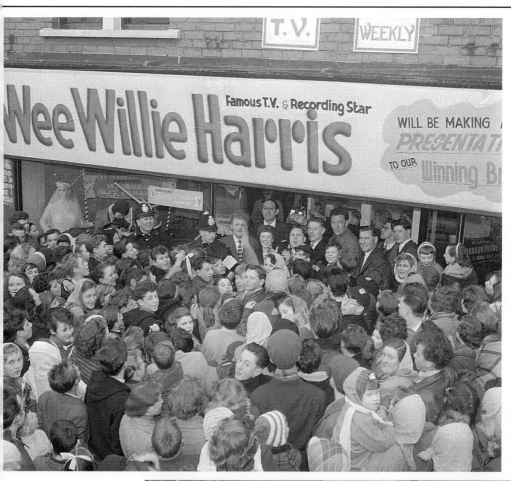

The crowd flocked to to the doors to get as close a view of their visiting celebrity, who can be seen flanked by Police officers for his own protection. The lower shot show Wee Willie Harris signing autographs inside the shop.
2584 Series. 14/3/58.

A publicity photograph of the National Provincial Bank branch which was situated on the corner of High Street and Lockwood Road. The bank started its' life in 1833, with an office in Threadneedle Street, London. Rapid growth was experienced during the Victorian and Edwardian eras as trade developed worldwide. Slower but consistent growth continued to the point where the bank became part of the National Westminster Bank group. The branch featured in this photograph is now closed and "Nat West" are to be found at 2 Barnsley Road, Goldthorpe. *4231. 21/5/60.*

Two heavy cranes from Mobile Lifting Services, raising the large conveyor gantry into place at Goldthorpe colliery. This conveyor transported coal from the drift to waiting coal wagons of the Dearne Valley Line. Goldthorpe colliery commenced operations in 1910, working on the Shafton seam which was 65 yards below the surface. Originally small shafts served the mine, but in 1956 a drift was driven for 2000 yards to allow the output of the pit to be extracted by mechanical conveyors. The original owners of the mine were Harry Lodge & Co who operated the mine until nationalisation. This colliery ceased production in 1994. Today, there is little to show that there was ever a colliery at Goldthorpe. *18134. 6/6/68.*

This view was commissioned by Dearne Council to support their arguments at a forthcoming demolition hearing. These brick houses were first built to house workers coming into the village following the opening of Hickleton Main colliery.

Before the sinking of the pit, Thurnscoe was a small farming community with the majority of the buildings being of stone. *1326. 13/12/55.*

The Thurnscoe branch of the Midland Bank on Station Road. Like many of the large clearing banks, 'The Midland' is the result of a long string of mergers with smaller banks including the Huddersfield Bank Inc. This Midland branch still operates from the same premises, those once occupied by Gallons are now vacant. *19903. 15/1/69.*

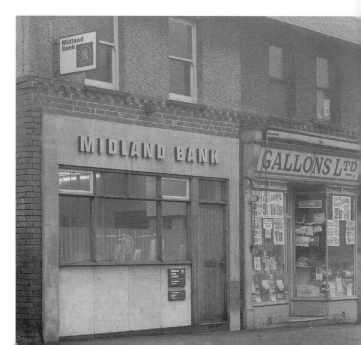

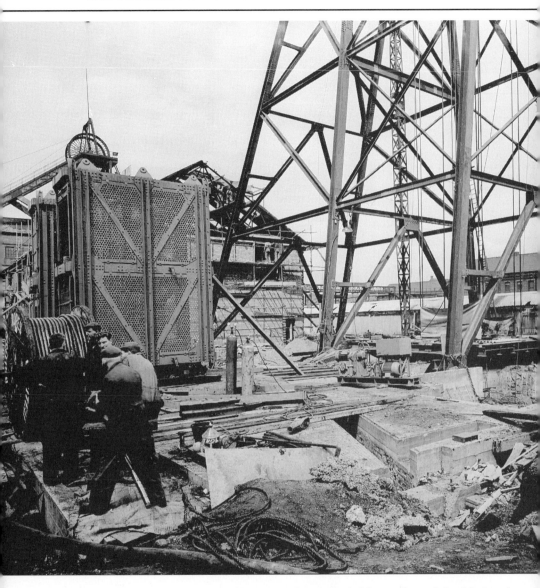

During the great drive to improve the pits in the South Yorkshire region of the National Coal Board during the late 50's and early 60's, many large projects were completed. Here, a team from Norwest Construction are about to install a new cage in the coal winder at Hickleton Main. *5169. 28/7/61.*

The newly installed conveyor system awaits the fitting of the belt upon which the coal is carried away to the waiting railway wagons. *5170. 28/7/61.*

Internal view of the winding shed with the winding gear main drum on the left of the photograph. The cable on this drum was the subject of frequent examination and it was regularly replaced for safety reasons. *5171. 28/7/61.*

The early stages of the installation of the new coal conveyor system at Hickleton Main colliery. The construction crew are from Norwest Construction. *5173. 28/7/61.*

A Coles crane operated by Mobile Lifting Services was brought in to raise heavy girders produced by Steel Engineering Products Ltd to the top of the new skip shaft framework at Hickleton Main colliery. This pit was sunk in 1892 and the Barnsley seam was worked from there for the following 63 years. In the 1920's the Parkgate seam was reached and this increased the manpower level of the pit to such an extent that by the mid 1930's, it employed in excess of 4,100 men, of whom approximately 3,300 worked underground. The annual output of the pit was often in excess of one million tons. From opening in 1892 until 1988, the Duncil, Newhill, Melton Field, Parkgate and Thorncliffe seams were worked from Hickleton Main. In 1994, the shafts were filled in and all the surface buildings demolished.

Until the 1880's, Thurnscoe was a small agricultural village, but with the sinking of the shafts at Hickleton Main, thousands of migrant mining families from surrounding areas converged on Thurnscoe seeking work in the pit, swelling the population to many times the pre 1880 level. *5023. 14/6/61.*

Most of the engineering work by Norwest Construction and their associated companies is now complete and Hickleton Main is ready to commence production at greatly enhanced levels. *5230. 17/8/61.*

N.C.B. wagons waiting to be filled with the first output from the updated Hickleton Main pit. The coal was delivered to these wagons already washed and ready for domestic or industrial use. *5235. 17/8/61.*

The new heapstead under construction at Kilnhurst Colliery. Work is well under way and much steel reinforcing is in place ready for concrete to be poured. In the distance can be seen the Martian like structure of an electricity pylon, representing one of the coal industry's largest customers.

The pit was sunk in 1859 and until 1924 it was operated by J & J Charlesworth and Company, who eventually sold the pit, along with its' associated brickworks, to Stuart and Lloyd Ltd. The brickworks closed in 1975 and the last coal was mined at Kilnhurst in 1989. *2294. 1/7/57.*

More modernisation work in progress at Kilnhurst colliery. The area in the foreground of this photograph is now the site occupied by Charles Thompson Fabrications. *2295. 1/7/57.*

The modern, by the standards of the day, reception area of the Danish Bacon Company. Despite the heavy headset and microphone, the receptionis still manages a beaming smile for her visitor. *2148. 24/3/57.*

'We'll meat again !' Inevitably the battle cry of the staff at Danish Bacon as the seemingly endless supply of joints arrive, to be prepared for shipment to the multitude of retailers large and small throughout Yorkshire.

Since it's formation as an English company, the Danish Bacon Company has always had a mixture of Danish and British directors. In the 1930's the turnover of the company was as high as nine million pounds per year. The close proximity of Kilnhurst to the motorway system and hence to the North Sea ports made South Yorkshire and particularly Kilnhurst, an excellent base for the company.

Ellis Robinson the Yorkshire cricketer, worked at the Kilnhurst plant following his retirement from professional cricket. *2149. 24/3/57.*

Yet another load of bacon sides being unloaded at Kilnhurst following a long run and sea voyage in the refrigerated lorry. The throughput of the plant was such that wagons were constantly unloading. *9919. 28/5/68.*

The Bedford truck fleet operated by the Danish Bacon Company Limited are lined up military fashion, with their drivers at the ready. This photograph was commissioned by the Michelin Tyre Company, who had the contract to supply tyre services to the fleet at that time. *2151. 23/4/57.*

The newly installed stage and lighting system at Westville Working Mens Club. The drum set may leave a certain amount to be desired by modern standards, but without doubt Ringo Starr would have felt perfectly at home with such a modest setup. The Westville WMC has a long history and has always been known for high standards which supported loyal and numerous membership. The club remains a popular meeting place. *15052. 11/12/67.*

Edward Smith & Sons Ltd sold high quality garments and knitwear in West Melton for many years. Special journeys from adjoining areas were frequently made in order to examine and hopefully purchase the latest and best quality garments. Sadly the shop is no longer trading. *7282. 3/10/63.*

The interior of the 'Rockingham Arms', showing off its' traditional bar. Historically the 'bar' was a heavy plank or metal bar which served as a very real demarcation line between the landlord and his, hopefully, ever thirsty customers. *37947. 17/11/75.*

The ivy clad exterior of the Rockingham Arms today. *Photograph courtesy of the Rockingham Arms.*

This photograph was taken for Swinton Urban District Council for use in support of an application for a demolition order on the street. Note the traditional 'corner shop', only in this case it is in the middle of the row of houses. This street ran off Queen Street and was eventually demolished, along with many others, to enable Ben Bailey Plc to construct more modern housing on the same ground. This was to become the Cresswell Estate. In more recent times this type of redevelopment of land which has already been built on once, has become fashionable again. These days we call it a 'brown field site'. *3355. 2/3/59.*

A rear view of houses on Albert Street, showing the enclosed communal yard which in this case served three houses. This is typical of the 'workers housing' erected in the second half of the nineteenth century. *3356. 2/3/59.*

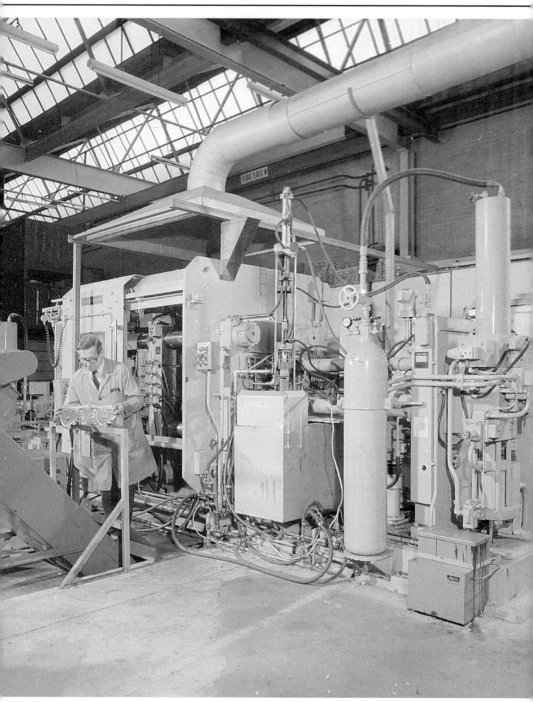

At the GEC plant, we see the newly installed Castmaster 500 machine. This machine manufactured by Castmaster Ltd, of Chesterfield, cast aluminium parts for cookers. The installation of this machine made the production process much more cost effective. *C35311. 7/5/74.*

This photograph of Swinton Secondary Modern School was taken for Wade Construction soon after completion. Though the school had a sixth form from 1960 and having been purpose built as a Comprehensive, it did not formally open as a such until July 1962. *4585. 15/11/60.*

Swinton Day Training College soon after completion. Within a year these buildings were to become part of Swinton Comprehensive School. Little has changed over the years, with the possible exception that in this photograph there are no signs of vandalism. *5261. 21/8/61.*

A superb photograph of the final quality control and testing area of the GEC plant. The cookers made their way robot like on the conveyor system, gradually progressing towards completion and final examination. In the early 60's, demand was such that most manufacturers opened soon after Christmas and the New Year, though a boisterous event, brought little respite from work. *4651. 29/12/60.*

Two more willing workers carrying out the final stages of assembly at the GEC plant and no doubt wondering what to do with those last few mince pies and what was left of the turkey!

The G.E.C. company had been in the town since the late 1940's, when it took over an empty factory which during the war years had produced munitions. GEC was formed in 1900, with it's head office being Magnet House, Kingsway. London.

During the immediate post war years, the GEC cooker factory in Birmingham, was experiencing great difficulty in recruiting staff. Probably as a result of the better pay and conditions in the motor industry, which used the same skills a GEC. The board of GEC decided to open a factory in Swinton. The first cooker left the Swinton factory on the 27th of June 1946. The site, which is currently operated by Glen Dimplex, covers 24 acres with 400,000 square feet of workshop floor space. At its height the plant employed 1,200 people. *4652. 29/12/60.*

This photograph was commissioned by Hattersley Brothers to illustrate the modern methods used in the manufacture of their 'Vulcan' boilers. Their factory was the Queens foundry situated on Whitelee Road. An interesting bit of engineering history in this photograph is the overhead shaft mounted high on the back wall of the workshop. This system of having one master shaft from which all machinery was driven is as old as the water wheel and came to great prominence in the 19th century,when steam engines were introduced to power manufacturing machines, in particular lathes.

Hattersley Brothers was started by brothers Thomas and Charles in 1864, operating from a small workshop in Queen Street. In 1869 the company moved to the site featured in this shot and at its peak covered a ten acre site and manufactured such diverse products as fire grates and railway wheels. At its height the company had a staff of 300. The foundry closed in the 1970's after over 100 years of business. *4131. 6/4/61.*

A William Stones tanker transfers beer produced at their Cadum Road brewery in Sheffield, into containers at the Rowms Lane depot of Ward & Sons (Swinton) Ltd, where it would be either bottled or barelled.

Ward & Sons(Swinton) Ltd was started in 1874 by William Ward. In 1900 the company secured a contract to bottle for Bass & Worthington breweries which it held for many years. At its peak the company employed a staff of 120 people. They ceased trading in the 1970's. *2208. 3/10/61.*

The old bottling plant at Ward & Sons (Swinton) Ltd. Note the platform on which the staff stand and their 'wellies'. In both cases, these were necessary to protect them from the rivers of pop which flowed across the floors during bottling operations. This plant had the capacity to fill and cap 7,000 bottles per hour. *4460. 5/9/60.*

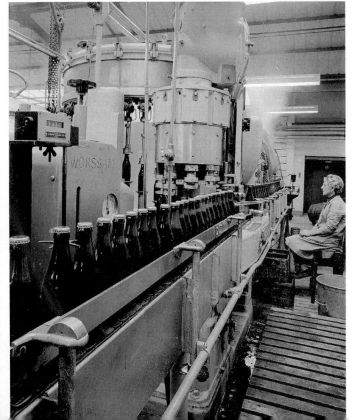

Opening day at Wards new bottling plant, which was able to bottle and label beer and soft drinks at a rate of 8,000 per hour. The raised platform was still there, but the 'wellies' would seem to be a thing of the past. *5627. 8/12/61.*

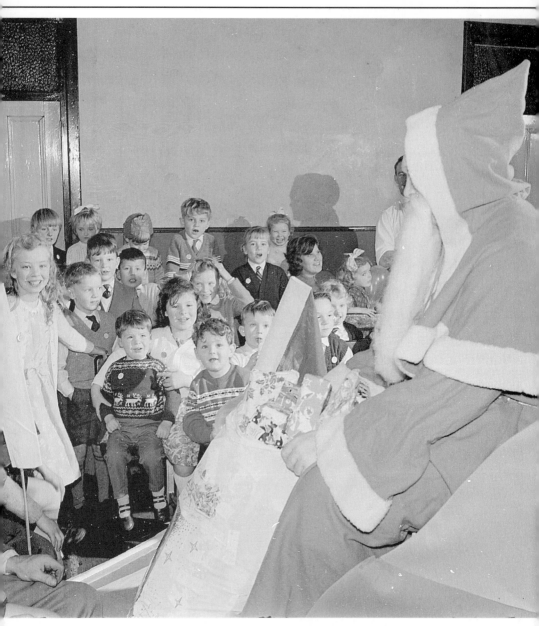

The Bridge Street Methodist Church Christmas party is in full swing and Father Christmas has the undivided attention of the assembled children.

Anyone recognise themselves or old friends in this shot?

Originally built in 1869 and demolished in the early 1970's, the church was situated on ground which is now the seated rest area on the right hand side as you go up Bridge Street. Such was the strength of Methodism in Swinton in the 19th century, that a further church was built in 1873 on Milton Street. *8751. 12/12/64.*

A team from Simon Carves Ltd engaged in the demolition of the old steam winder chimney at Manvers Main colliery. Noteworthy in this photograph is the seeming complete absence of safety equipment for the men.
Originally sunk in 1870, the pit remained productive until the 1980's. Before nationalisation, the colliery was owned by the Earl of Manvers who resided at Thoresby Hall. *1182. 9/9/55.*

Kier Construction required a photographic record of their work at Manvers Main collier during the improvement programme in the mid fifties. This was one of Mike Walters first commercial projects. Thousands of tons of steel and concrete went into the construction of the coal preparation plant at Manvers Main, at the time, one of the largest in the country. *10. July 1954.*

January 1957 was an apalling month for the companies working on the improvement scheme at Manvers Main, with torrential rain which left the site virtually impossible to work on. Certainly it was impassable for the heavy plant which was vital for the work to progress at the required rate. Mitchell Construction engaged Mike to take a series of photographs to support their argument that delays were the result of an 'act of God'. Without acceptance of their argument, they would have been liable for crippling penalty clauses under their contractual agreement with the National Coal Board.
2054 & 2056. 7/2/57.

With the construction of the coking plant well under way, we see here the condenser beginning to take shape. In the background can be seen the **Staithes** pub. *172. 2/7/58*

The main battery of coking ovens in the coking plant begin turning coal into coke. Rams pushed the product down the incline into the quelching pit. It was said that living in the shadow of Manvers was equivalent to smoking five or six cigarettes a day. After it's closure, the area was to become a smokeless zone. *1936. 24/11/56.*

Once washed and prepared, the coal is transferred into these huge hoppers which are positioned over the tracks carrying the special coal trucks. Once loaded, the trucks formed what were known as 'coal liner trains', which delivered the vital fuel to steelworks and power stations, the key customers for the coal industry.
2215. 6/5/57.

The power distribution centre was situated on the lower level of the Coal Preparation Plant. A specially installed supply had to be constructed feeding straight from the National Grid. Truly electrifying.
2251. 18/5/57.

A general view of the Manvers Main Central Coal Processing Plant taken immediately following completion of the modernisation programme. This plant washed coal drawn from Manvers, Wath, Barnburgh and Kilnhurst pits.

On a visit to the plant in the 1970's, the author was astounded at the high noise level and constant vibration, which could be felt virtually everywhere on the site. The manager at the time of my visit was Ted Lunness, who stayed with the plant until its eventual closure along with Manvers Main colliery. The site is now home to a growing number of high tech companies and with the opening of the Dearne Valley Link in 1998, the area is designated to be a major factor in the re-generation of the area after the decline of the coal industry. *2342. August 1957.*

The coke ovens in operation. The high pressure jet was necessary to clean the surfaces between baking operations. This photograph was taken for the Plybrico Co Ltd, the makers of the oven linings.
049. 17/6/63.

The Area Face Control Room was situated at Manvers Main but monitored the performance of all the collieries in the area. As can be seen, the various pits controlled are listed alphabetically round the room. This centre was manned twenty four hours a day and constantly monitored the performance of each face.
Production managers from all the pits covered would regularly check with the centre as to the relative performance of their pits. In the event of a major breakdown, this centre would be responsible for calling out the necessary staff to correct the situation, regardless of the time of day, or night.
9750. 29/10/65.

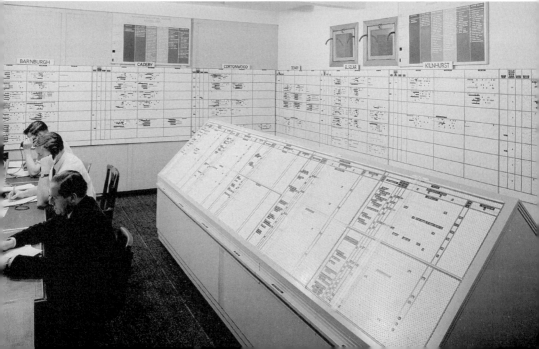

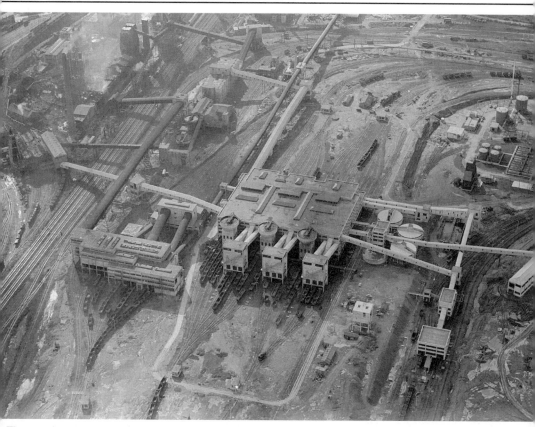

Two aerial photographs of the Manvers Main site taken from a light aircraft hired by the NCB for the purpose. In both shots, the dominant feature is the new Coal Processing Plant and the huge hoppers which dispensed coal into the wagons passing beneath them. At the top right of shot number 7735 (above), can be seen the Dearne and Don canal. *77731 & 7735. 3/4/64.*

Wath colliery showing the chimneys and steam powered winders still in place.
The pit, originally sunk in 1876 to a depth of 382 yards, was deepened in 1912 to reach the high quality coal of the Parkgate seam. During the life of the pit, coal was also extracted from the Barnsley, Swallowood, Newhill and Melton seams.
In the late 1950's, the pit was connected by a diesel roadway to Manvers Main colliery, from where coal mined at Wath was brought to the surface. The last coal was mined at Wath in 1986 and just prior to closure, some 400,000 tons per year was produced.
1931. 24/11/56.

Mike was contracted to record for posterity the completion of the newly modernised town centre. The redevelopment was considered to be extremely modern at the time. Clearly, pedestrianisation was still a policy for the future.
33157. 13/2/73.

The Midland Bank in Montgomery Road immediately after its refurbishment. With the minor differences of new lettering and signs, the bank looks very much the same now as it did then.

The Midland Bank opened for business in Birmingham in 1836. As it developed it absorbed numerous regional banks including the Sheffield Union Bank in 1901 and the Sheffield and Hallamshire Bank in 1913.
19902. 15/1/69.

The modern shop fronts on Montgomery Square. In the background can be seen the Midland Bank which faces onto Montgomery Road. The precinct is now fully pedestrianised with the by-pass taking traffic (and trade) away from the town centre. 33158. 13/2/73.

PARKGATE IRON & STEEL WORKS LTD.

The Parkgate Iron & Steel Company started life in 1823, when two Sheffield entrepreneurs thought the demand for iron was on the increase and a new company could flourish. They chose the Parkgate site for two fundamental reasons. The plentiful supply of locally mined coal and the ease of access to the South Yorkshire Canal which flanked the site. In 1832 the founders interests were bought out and the company was renamed 'The Birmingham Tin Plate Company'. By 1839 a blast furnace had been installed which increased output of higher grades of steel. In 1840 the company again changed hands, this time being bought by the three man partnership of William Schofield, Charles Geach and Samuel Beale.

The nationwide expansion of the railway system increased the demand for steel and in 1845 a new mill to produce rails was installed. Following the death of one partner and the departure of another, the company became Samuel Beale and Company in 1854. In 1856 the company commenced the production of armour plating for warships, hence ensuring continuing expansion.

Samuel Beale retired in 1864 and placed the company in the hands of his son Lansdowne Beale. Lansdowne incorporated the company and changed its name to the 'Parkgate Iron Company Limited.

In 1871, two more blast furnaces were installed, adding to the development of the already considerable size of the works. During major redevelopment in 1888, a billet mill, slab mill, large plate mill and three twenty five ton capacity open hearth furnaces were added. To take account of the change in the products produced by the company, it was renamed the Parkgate Iron & Steel Company Limited. In1905 two more new blast furnaces were installed and the first ever three high plate mill was added in 1906.

Changes in the demands of the market meant that the company began to concentrate its efforts into production of steel bar, utilising new rolling mill technology. Simultaneously, more land was purchased at Roundwood to acommodate further expansion. In 1920, the tenth open hearth furnace was installed, along with 12″ and 24″ mills. By 1953, plate manufacture had ceased, being replaced by a continuous bar mill which was commissioned that year.

Following the deaths of the remaining family shareholders, the company was put up for sale and the majority of the shares were acquired by Tube Investments Limited. Following a review of the operations of the company by the new board, it was decided to add wire production to the capacity of the plant. Part of the works was demolished in February 1961 and construction began on a new 42″ reversing bloom mill. This work was completed in 1963. By 1964 the continuous narrow strip mill was operating alongside a new billet and primary mill. In all some 6,000 men were employed on the site and two hundred and fifty different grades of steel were being supplied to customers at home and overseas.

Raw steel was supplied to tube manufacturers, hot and cold forgers, bright steel drawers, heavy and light engineering as well as cycle, vehicle and aircraft manufacturers.

The slow but steady demise of the plant began in the early 1970's when parts of the plant fell into disuse and were demolished. What remained of the Parkgate site was finally closed by 1982. The segment of the company which operated from the Aldwarke site was eventually absorbed into British Steel.

A group of mechanical engineering trainees at Parkgate being taught the rudiments of steel making. Note the model blast furnace. *7985. 27/4/64.*

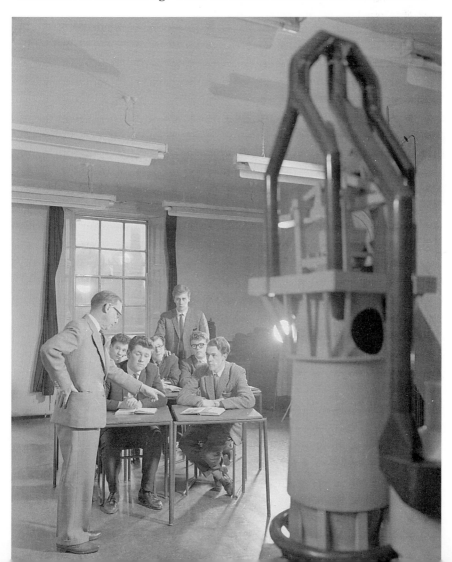

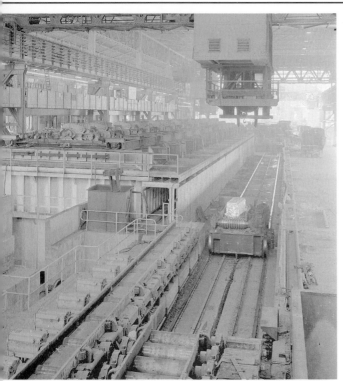

In this photograph we see an ingot being transported on a 'buggy'. This device was used to transport ingots around the plant. It was moved by a hawser pulling it along. *7894. 23/4/64.*

As they leave the primary mill, steel bars are being cut into manageable lengths by the Loewy cold shears. This operation is controlled by the operator who is standing at the control table. *7913. 17/4/64.*

These operators were transferring written or typed information onto punched tape for feeding data into the computer system, the company also had magnetic tape information storage and retrival systems at this time. Many of these girls also doubled up as 'Comptometer' operators. These machines had 80 to 100 buttons on the top, which when pressed down individually or in groups would perform complex calculations. *7737. 3/4/64.*

Molten steel being poured into moulds to form ingots. The molten metal was taken straight from the blast furnace. The contents of the moulds on the right are glowing hotly while the empty ones stand waiting to the left of the loading bucket. *7601. 28/2/64.*

The spectacular display as the Kaldo furnace contents are poured into the loading bucket. *7940. 19/4/64.*

H section girders being stacked for shipment. This remains the standard section used by the construction industry. *7693. 25/3/64.*

A Davey Brothers cutter being used to cut round bar. The cold shears used on other material were not suitable for this work as they tended to distort the bar causing waste. *7692. 25/3/64.*

The huge electro magnet which was used to pick up scrap, which was then added to the mixture in the blast furnaces. This recycled scrap formed a significant part of the mixture for many grades of steel. *8096. 8/5/64.*

The Kaldo control centre installed by English Electric. From here the operators carefully monitored all aspects of the steel making process. *7733. 3/4/64.*

Taking the temperature of the molten steel before pouring into the mould. The temperature was sensed by a thermocouple in the end of the lance and a signal was passed back up the lance and along the cable which can be seen trailing back from the operators handgrip. Pouring at the correct temperature was critical to the quality of the steel. *7750. 3/4/64.*

Once molten steel has reached a furnace temperature of 1,600 degrees centigrade, it is ready to be poured into ingot moulds. Once solidified and cooled, the ingots will weigh between 3.5 and 4 tons each, depending on the type of steel being cast. *7920. 18/4/64.*

Potential trainees in their last year at school are given an introductory tour of the mill. It was a regular part of the company strategy to introduce potential trainees and apprentices to the industry. *12312. 17/5/67.*

A fine photograph of the two blast furnaces at Parkgate, towering over the works and the surrounding area. These furnaces were capable of a combined output of 2,500 tons of iron per week. The smaller furnace measured 14 ft 6 inches in diameter, the larger 15 ft 6 inches. Most of the output from these furnaces was used in the Kaldo pneumatic steel making process, which at the time was the most productive process in the world.
7520. 20/1/64.

The internal railway system serving Parkgate and Aldwarke sites was used to transport iron and steel in molten form between the sites and finished steel, via the British Rail link direct to customers. *8088. 8/5/64.*

A mixture of iron being poured into the Kaldo unit for purification into steel. *7955. 19/4/64.*

Every batch of steel was subjected to careful testing and analysis to ensure it conformed to the customer's specification. Among other things were tests for tensile strength, crack resistance and carbon content. *14100. 29/9/67.*

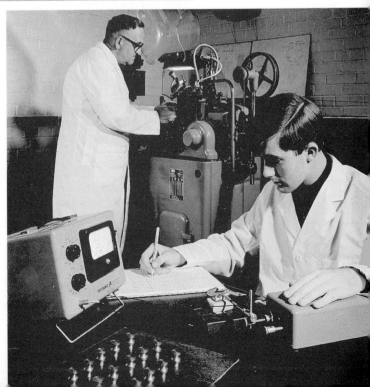

One of the three canteens which operated in different parts of the plant. These supplied meals and snacks at subsidised prices and the staff had a clean and modern environment in which to take their meal breaks. *7712. 27/3/64.*

The newly modernised reception area where all visitors were greeted on arrival.
Just the image that a major company would wish to present to visiting customers and suppliers alike. On the wall behind the receptionists seat can be seen a plaque which bore a brief history of the company. Is there anyone who knows where it is now ?
10055. 27/3/66.

This aerial view of the old and new works at Parkgate give an excellent impression of the extent of the plant. Also the internal road and rail systems can be clearly seen. An excellent reference shot for aspiring railway modellers. *8276. 20/6/64.*

Trainee mechanical engineers at work in the 'practical' workshop. At this time major companies took great pride in the thoroughness of their training programmes. 7601/138. 2/3/64.

A typical New Year's Eve scene in the ingot storage area where it was always, 'business as usual'. *8795. 31/12/64.*

A general view of the primary mill in the process of producing the seemingly endless suppy of steel bar. *7601/95. 2/3/65.*

A fifty ton trailer, drawn by what looks very muc[h] like an ex Army tank tractor, hauling a load of rectangular bars from the primary mill to the str[ip] mill for further processing. *8121. 14/5/64.*

One of the fleet of ERF tipper lorries delivering material directly into a hopper, from where it will pass directly to the furnaces. A large fleet of these lorries were used to transport material from on site dumps to where it was needed. *8007. 24/4/64.*

A diesel locomotive and two flasks of molten iron silhouetted against the sky in an emotive photograph taken in the heyday of steelmaking at Parkgate. *7601/182. 2/3/64.*

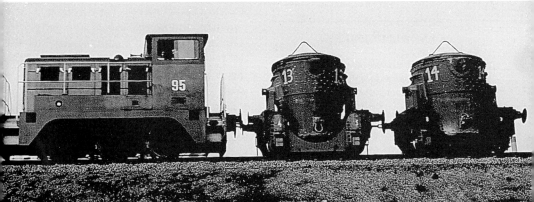

Giles Brearley *(on the left)* is a Chartered Management Accountant in practice in Swinton. He was born at Barnsley, but resided at Mexborough. He went to college at High Melton, Doncaster, Sheffield and York. His father was Chief Public Health Inspector for Mexborough from 1940 until 1974. Giles has written other local history books – *Mexborough A Town At War* and *We Will Remember,* (jointly with Graham Oliver) and also wrote *History of Lead Mining in the Peak District* which was based on his years potholing in Derbyshire as a student.

ACKNOWLEDGEMENTS.

The authors would like to offer their thanks to those without whose assistance this book would not have been possible, among whom are:

Pat Walters
Roy Wooding
Fred Gray
Diane Walters
The Laird of Camster for his South Yorkshire Notes
Graham Oliver

Paul Walters *(on the right)* began his professional career as a photographer in 1987. When he joined his father's company at the age of 24. His first task in learning the trade, was to assist Michael on a ten country tour of Europe for a multi-national company. It was this marathon 10,000 mile race around the continent that moulded the direction of Paul's career. Initially working with his father covering major building projects in addition to publications such as the APA guide to Athens, Michael managed to teach Paul not only the practical basics, but how to approach a subject to bring out its best characteristics. They worked together until he was forced into early retirement due to ill health. Michael would use people to bring a subject to life and this is a technique Paul still uses in his work today.

Paul now spends much of his time overseas working for major travel companies, producing photographs for holiday brochures in addition to his UK based work in the production of pictures and exhibitions for Industry and Commerce